WITHDRAWN

PRO
BASEBALL'S
CHAMPIONSHIP

BY TYLER OMOTH

CAPSTONE PRESS
a capstone imprint

Blazers Books are published by Capstone Press,
1710 Roe Crest Drive, North Mankato, Minnesota 56003
www.mycapstone.com

Library of Congress Cataloging-in-Publication Data
Names: Omoth, Tyler, author.
Title: Pro baseball's championship / by Tyler Omoth.
Description: North Mankato, Minnesota : An imprint of Capstone Press, [2018]
    | Series: Major Sports Championships | Series: Blazers | Audience: Ages:
    8-14.
Identifiers: LCCN 2017028552 (print) | LCCN 2017033685 (ebook) | ISBN
    9781543505214 (eBook PDF) | ISBN 9781543504972 (hardcover)
Subjects: LCSH: World Series (Baseball)—History—Juvenile literature. |
    American League Championship Series (Baseball)—Juvenile literature. |
    National League Championship Series (Baseball)—Juvenile literature. |
    Baseball—History—Juvenile literature.
Classification: LCC GV878.4 (ebook) | LCC GV878.4 .O56 2018 (print) | DDC
    796.357/646—dc23
LC record available at https://lccn.loc.gov/2017028552

Editorial Credits
Carrie Braulick Sheely, editor; Kyle Grenz, designer; Eric Gohl, media researcher;
Kathy McColley, production specialist

Photo Credits
Dreamstime: Jerry Coli, 8; Getty Images: Bettmann, 9, 23, Focus On Sport, 27, New
York Daily News Archive, 24, Stringer/Rick Stewart, 18, 29; Library of Congress: 7;
Newscom: AFLO, 4–5, Icon SMI/SI/John Biever, 17 (top), Icon Sportswire/Patrick
Gorski, cover; MCT/Ron T. Ennis, 21, Reuters/Mike Segar, 17 (bottom), Reuters/Ray
Stubblebine, 11, UPI/Kevin Dietsch, 14, ZUMA Press/Chris Young, 12–13

Design Elements: Shutterstock

Printed and bound in the USA.
010754S18

TABLE OF CONTENTS

A LONG WAIT FOR A WIN

It was Game 7 of the 2016 World Series. The Chicago Cubs and Cleveland Indians were tied in the 10th inning. The Cubs scored two runs, and then held off the Indians. The Cubs won! They hadn't won the title since 1908.

The Cubs celebrate their 2016 World Series win.

FACT According to a legend, a man named Bill Sianis cursed the Cubs in 1945. He was upset because he wasn't allowed to bring his billy goat to a game.

HISTORY OF THE WORLD SERIES

In 1903 the Pittsburgh Pirates had a big lead in the National League (NL). In the American League (AL), the Boston Americans were a top team. The NL and AL teams never played each other. But fans wanted to see that happen.

The Pittsburgh Pirates baseball team began in 1891.
Before that time, the team was known as Allegheny.

FACT Only two teams in Major League Baseball (MLB) have never made it to the World Series. These teams are the Seattle Mariners and the Washington Nationals.

FACT In the 1903 World Series, balls hit into the fans who lined the **outfield** were ruled **ground-rule** triples. There were a record 25 triples in the series.

The 1903 World Series was played at Huntington Avenue ballfield in Boston, Massachusetts.

outfield—the grassy area beyond where the bases are placed

ground rule—a rule that applies to an individual baseball park; if a fair ball can't be played by a fielder, ground rules determine the number of bases the batter is awarded

The two teams' owners planned a matchup they called the World Series. The teams faced off on October 1, 1903. It was an instant hit. More than 16,000 fans watched the game. Boston won the first World Series.

THE *ROAD* TO THE WORLD SERIES

The World Series has always been a matchup of the AL and NL **pennant** winners. But the way the teams get there has changed. Today six **division** winners and four **wild card** teams go to the playoffs.

Derek Jeter holds the World Series trophy as he celebrates with teammates after the New York Yankees' 2009 World Series win.

pennant—a triangular flag that symbolizes a league championship

division—a small group of teams in a league that compete against one another; divisions are often grouped by location

wild card—a team that advances to the playoffs without winning a division

MOST WORLD SERIES CHAMPIONSHIPS

TEAM	WINS
NEW YORK YANKEES	27
ST. LOUIS CARDINALS	11
BOSTON RED SOX	8

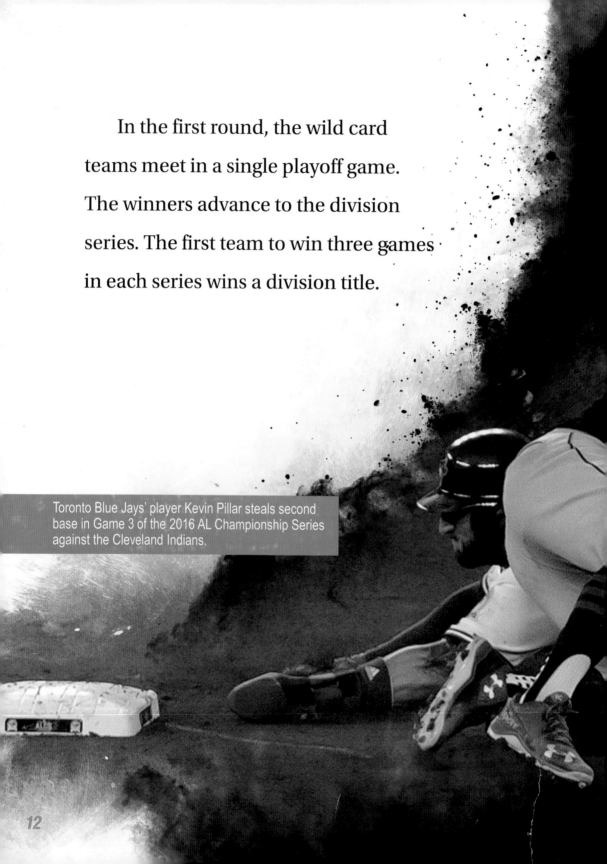

In the first round, the wild card teams meet in a single playoff game. The winners advance to the division series. The first team to win three games in each series wins a division title.

Toronto Blue Jays' player Kevin Pillar steals second base in Game 3 of the 2016 AL Championship Series against the Cleveland Indians.

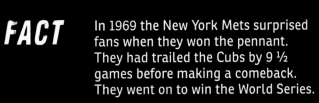

The division winners play in the AL and NL Championship Series. Finally, the two league champs meet in the World Series. The first team to win four of seven games earns the title.

MOST WORLD SERIES APPEARANCES

TEAM	APPEARANCES
NEW YORK YANKEES	40
LOS ANGELES DODGERS	18
SAN FRANCISCO GIANTS	18
ST. LOUIS CARDINALS	18
OAKLAND ATHLETICS	14

San Francisco Giants' player Michael Morse celebrates his hit that drove in a run during Game 7 of the 2014 World Series.

MEMORABLE MOMENTS

Fans remember some World Series even as the years pass. The 2001 series was close. In Game 7, the New York Yankees led the Arizona Diamondbacks 2-1. Yankees' star **closer** Mariano Rivera came to the mound. But Arizona still drove in two runs for the big win.

closer—a pitcher brought in during the late innings, usually to save the game

Luis Gonzalez smacks the World-Series-winning hit for the Diamondbacks in 2001.

FACT

The 2001 Diamondbacks' win broke a Yankees' winning streak. The Yankees had won the World Series in 1998, 1999, and 2000.

Luis Gonzalez celebrated his hit by jumping in the air at first base.

Jack Morris winds up to deliver a pitch during the 1991 World Series.

In 1991 the Minnesota Twins faced the Atlanta Braves. Three games went into extra innings. Game 7 was a pitchers' battle between the Braves' John Smoltz and the Twins' Jack Morris. The Twins finally scored in the 10th inning to win.

FACT In World Series history, only one pitcher has thrown a **perfect game**. New York Yankees' pitcher Don Larsen did it in Game 5 of the 1956 World Series.

perfect game—a game in which a pitcher doesn't allow a single batter to reach first base

In Game 6 in 2011, the St. Louis Cardinals were one **strike** away from defeat. Then Lance Berkman drove in the tying run. David Freese hit a heroic **walk-off home run** in the 11th inning for the win. The Cardinals beat the Texas Rangers in Game 7.

MOST CAREER WORLD SERIES HOME RUNS

PLAYER	HOME RUNS
MICKEY MANTLE	18
BABE RUTH	15
YOGI BERRA	12
DUKE SNIDER	11

strike—a pitched ball that is swung at and missed, a pitched ball that is in the strike zone but not swung at, or a pitched ball that is hit foul

walk-off home run—a game-winning home run in the bottom half of the last inning of a game

Teammates welcome David Freese at home plate after his game-winning hit in Game 6 of the 2011 World Series.

WORLD SERIES HEROES

PLAYER: BILL MAZEROSKI

WORLD SERIES: 1960

**TEAMS: PITTSBURGH PIRATES,
NEW YORK YANKEES**

GAME: 6

Some players are remembered for their World Series performances. In 1960 Game 6 was tied at the bottom of the 9th inning. Pirates' player Bill Mazeroski came to the plate. He slammed a walk-off home run for the win. It was the first in World Series history.

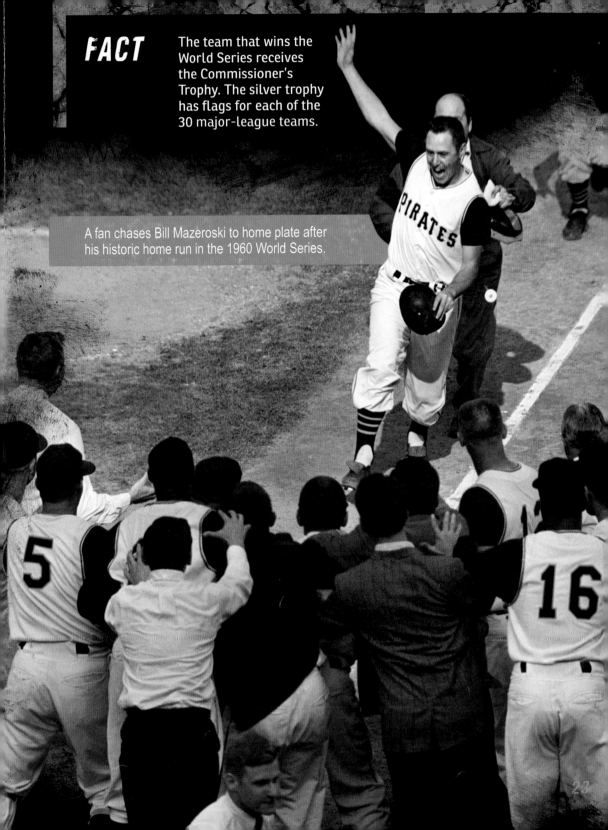

A fan chases Bill Mazeroski to home plate after his historic home run in the 1960 World Series.

PLAYER: REGGIE JACKSON

WORLD SERIES: 1977

TEAMS: LOS ANGELES DODGERS, NEW YORK YANKEES

GAME: 6

In 1977 the Yankees' Reggie Jackson put on a show in the fourth inning of Game 6. In three straight at bats, he smashed a home run on the first pitch.

Teammates welcome Reggie Jackson (right) after his first home run in Game 6 of the 1977 World Series.

FACT The World Series almost always is in October. After the 1977 World Series, Reggie Jackson became known as "Mr. October."

PLAYER: **KIRK GIBSON**

WORLD SERIES: *1988*

TEAMS: **LOS ANGELES DODGERS, OAKLAND ATHLETICS**

In 1988 in Game 1, the Athletics led the Dodgers. Injured Dodgers' player Kirk Gibson walked to the plate. He smashed a home run! The Dodgers won the game and later the title.

Kirk Gibson hits his home run during the 9th inning of Game 1 in the 1988 World Series.

PLAYER: JOE CARTER

WORLD SERIES: 1993

TEAMS: TORONTO BLUE JAYS, PHILADELPHIA PHILLIES

GAME: 6

In 1993 the Blue Jays trailed the Phillies 6-5 in Game 6. With two runners on base, Blue Jay Joe Carter blasted a home run. Carter skipped and jumped all the way to home plate. His homer made the Blue Jays the World Series champs.

Teammates hoist Joe Carter on their shoulders after his home run that won the Blue Jays the 1993 World Series.

Glossary

closer (KLOS-ur)—a pitcher brought in during the late innings, usually to save the game

division (di-VIZH-uhn)—a small group of teams in a league that compete against one another; divisions are often grouped by location

ground rule (GROUND ROOL)—a rule that applies to an individual baseball park; if a fair ball can't be played by a fielder, ground rules determine the number of bases the batter is awarded

legend (LEJ-uhnd)—a story passed down through the years that may not be completely true

outfield (OUT-feeld)—the grassy area beyond where the bases are placed

pennant (PEN-uhnt)—a triangular flag that symbolizes a league championship

perfect game (PUR-fikt GAME)—a game in which a pitcher doesn't allow a single batter to reach first base

strike (STRIKE)—a pitched ball that is swung at and missed, a pitched ball that is in the strike zone but not swung at, or a pitched ball that is hit foul

walk-off home run (WALK-off HOME RUN)—a game-winning home run in the bottom half of the last inning of a game

wild card (WILD KARD)—a team that advances to the playoffs without winning a division

Read More

Herman, Gail. *What Is the World Series?* What Is? New York: Grosset & Dunlap, 2015.

Osborne, Mary Pope, and Natalie Pope Boyce. *Baseball.* Fact Tracker. New York: Random House Children's Books, 2017.

Storden, Thom. *Amazing Baseball Records.* Epic Sports Records. North Mankato, Minn.: Capstone, 2015.

Internet Sites

Use FactHound to find Internet sites related to this book.

Visit *www.facthound.com*

Just type in **9781543504972** and go.

Check out projects, games and lots more at
www.capstonekids.com

Index